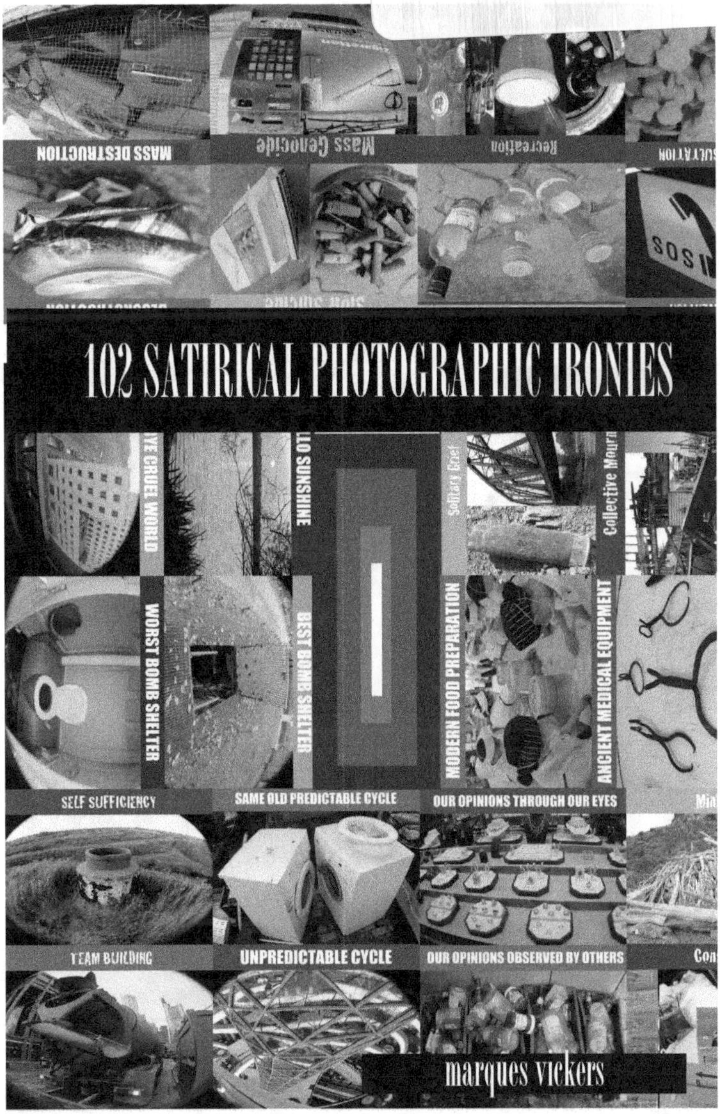
MASS DESTRUCTION
Mass Genocide
Recreation
102 SATIRICAL PHOTOGRAPHIC IRONIES
WORST BOMB SHELTER
BEST BOMB SHELTER
MODERN FOOD PREPARATION
ANCIENT MEDICAL EQUIPMENT
SELF SUFFICIENCY
SAME OLD PREDICTABLE CYCLE
OUR OPINIONS THROUGH OUR EYES
TEAM BUILDING
UNPREDICTABLE CYCLE
OUR OPINIONS OBSERVED BY OTHERS
marques vickers

102 Satirical Photographic Ironies
Subtle to Subversive

MARQUIS PUBLISHING
Herron Island, Washington

@2016 Marques Vickers

Version 1

Published by Marquis Publishing
Herron Island, Washington

Vickers, Marques, 1957

102 Satirical Photographic Ironies

Dedicated to my daughters Charline and Caroline

Preface

Irony and subtlety enable proper satire. The shrewder and more subversive the message, the greater the likelihood it will be misunderstood or unappreciated.

This photographic edition is an entertaining and disarming visual portrayal of lifestyle choices and realities that pose paradoxical contrasts. It is my third satirical work, this time venturing into social commentary. My two previous editions have concentrated on human phobias and obsessions.

Among the varied topics of assault include racism, sexism, nationalism, poverty, addiction, privacy invasion, societal evolution, icons, vanishing idealism, excess and clichés that often summarize human behavior.

I have attempted to keep my perspective succinct with an occasional bite that more likely resembles a nip. This tactic is employed contrary to professional overt proselytizing that is usually condescending, sentimentalized or simply redundant.

You may not always agree with my point of view, but I thank you for at least contemplating an alternative.

Slow Suicide

Recreation

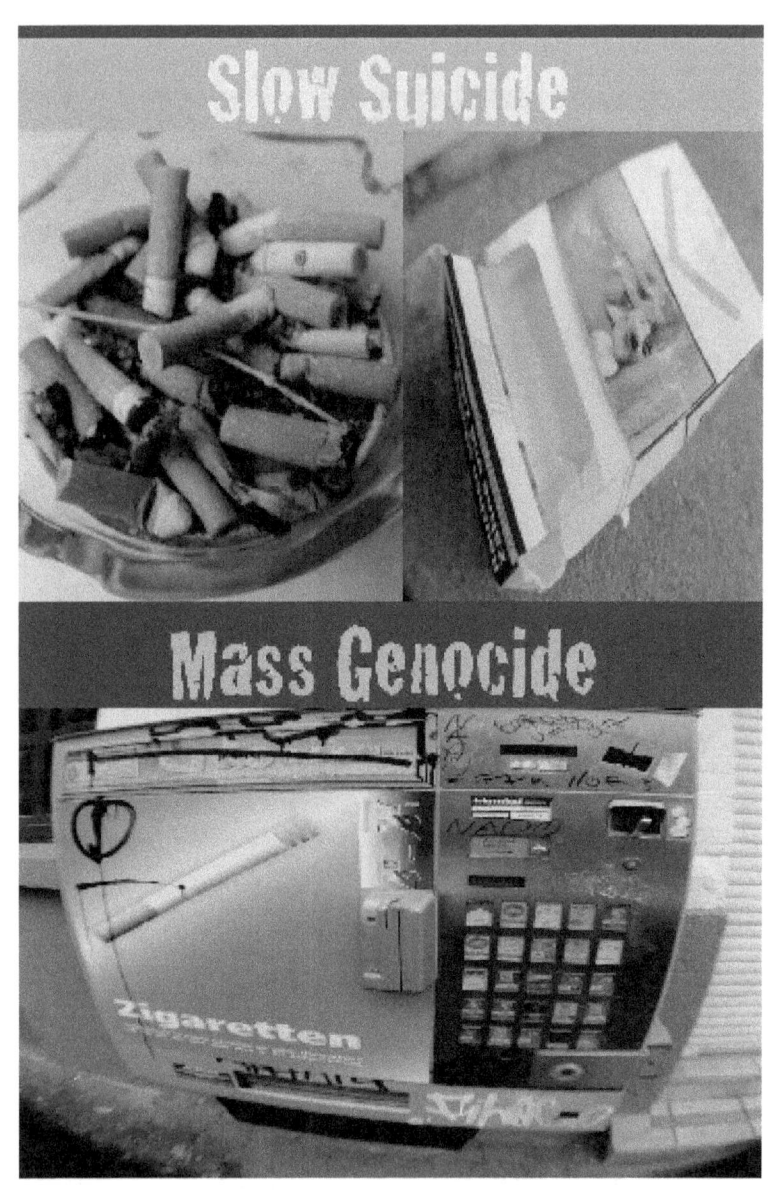

Solitary Grief

Collective Mourning

Solitary Grief

Collective Mourning

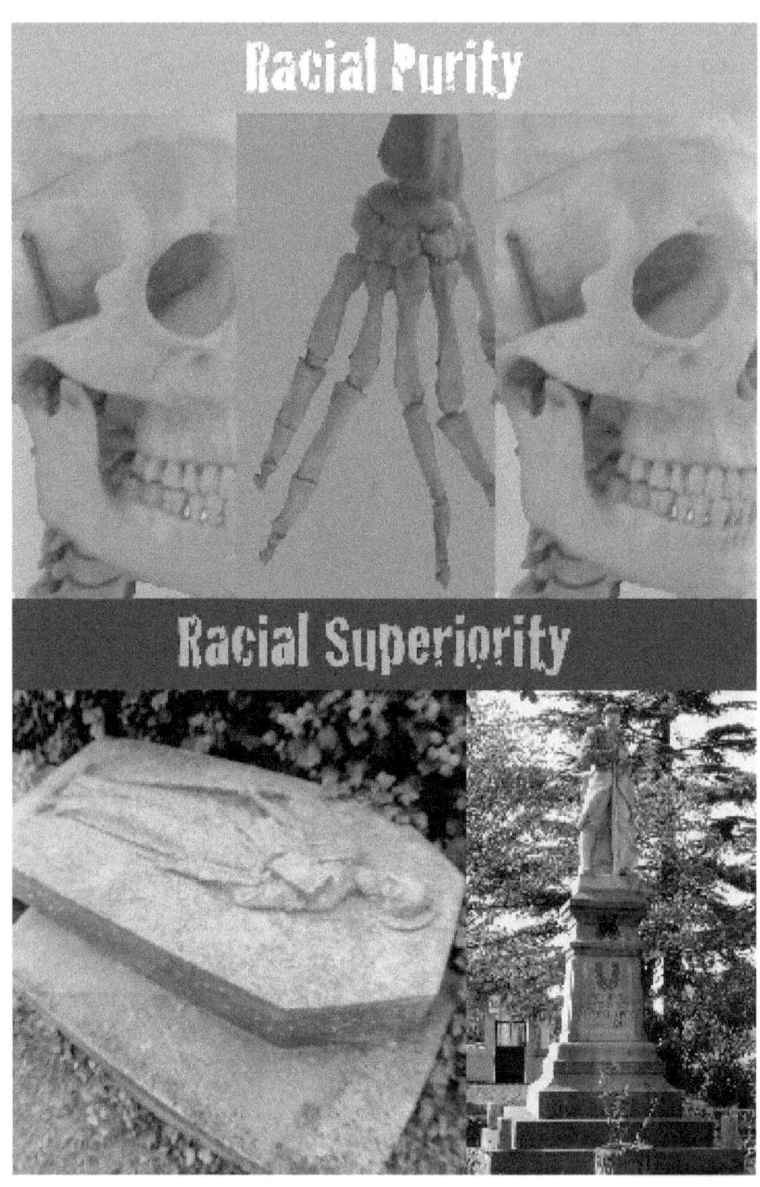

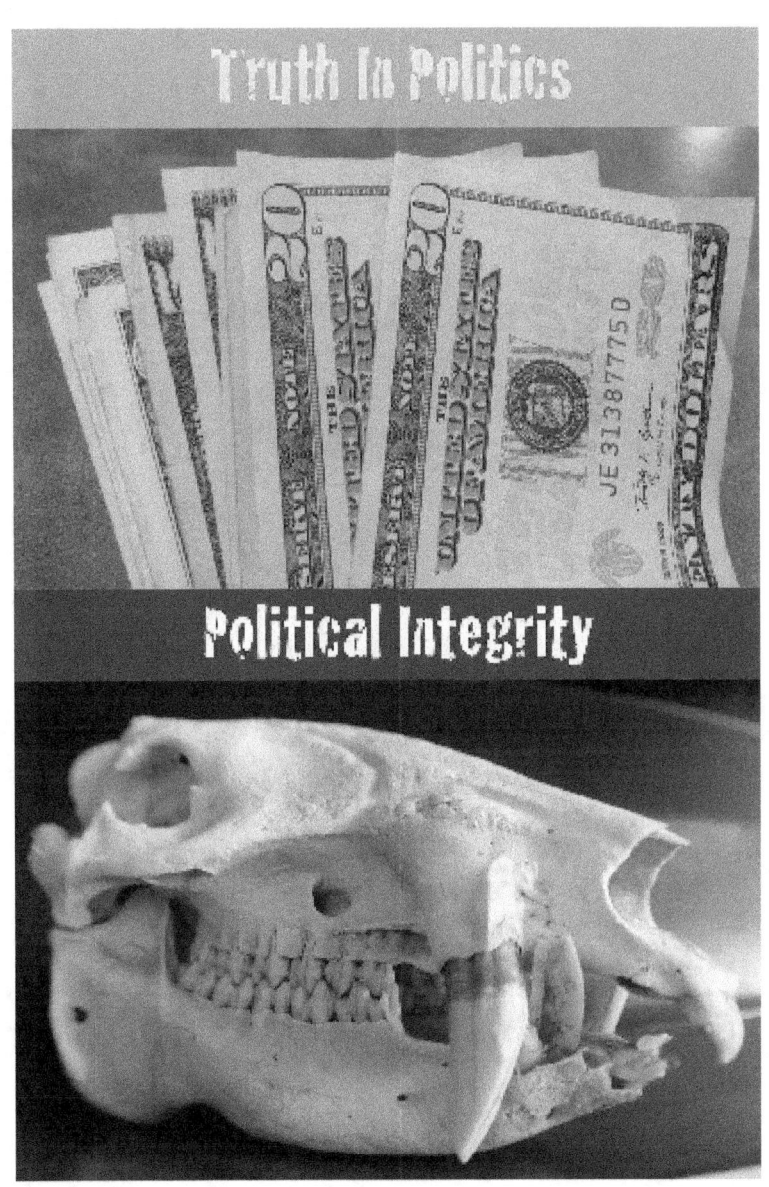

EXPECATIONS OF QUALITY

HOTELSTARS.EU

LOWERED EXPECTATIONS

PUBLIC CONSUMPTION

PRIVATE CONSUMPTION

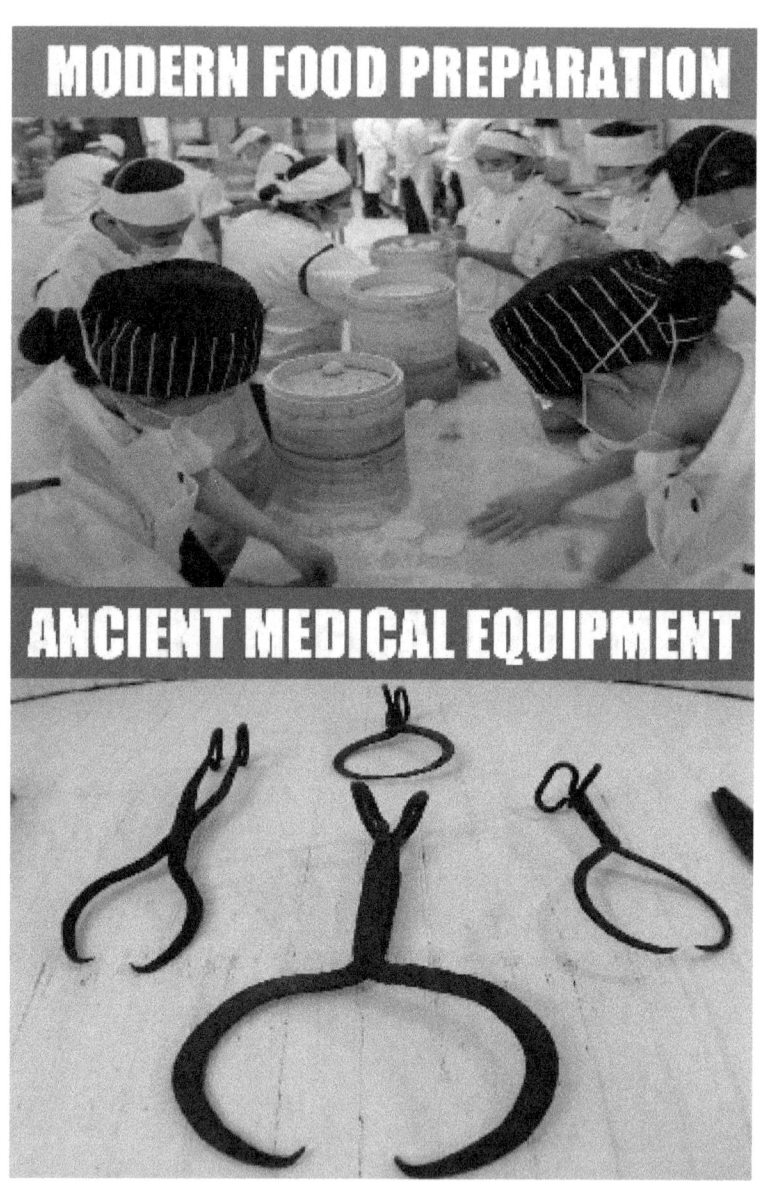

COARSE

ETERNAL

POOR IMPULSIVE INVESTMENT

FATAL IMPULSIVE DECISION

FLATTERING SUN POSITIONING

POOR SUN POSITIONING

WORST EARTHQUAKE SPOT

BEST EARTHQUAKE LOCATION

DOMESTICATED

SAVAGE

THE QUEST

INADEQUATE MEDIUM

SHELL OF A SHELL

AUTHENTIC REPLICA

ERECTILE DYSFUNCTION

EJACULATION

THE MADDING CROWD

SOLITUDE

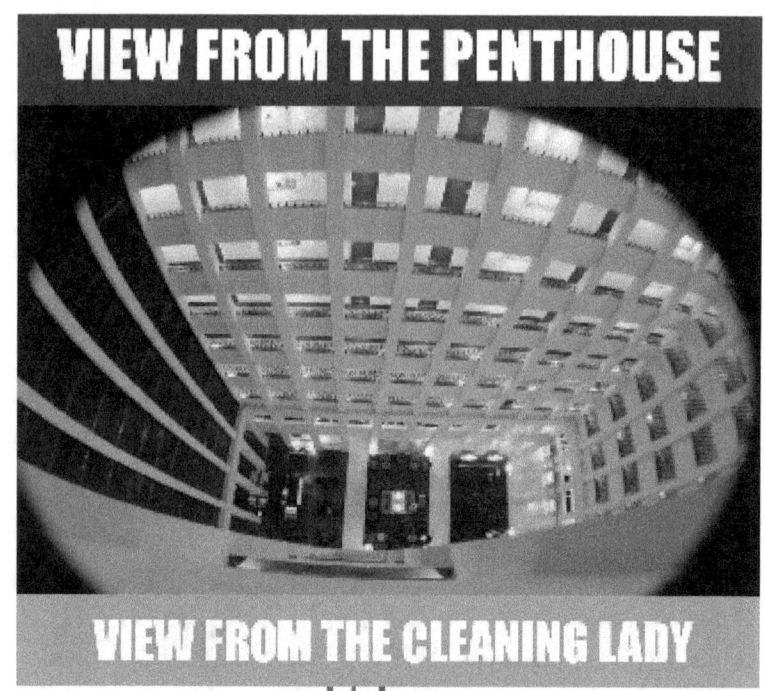

HOLOCAUST MEMORIAL

HIER WOHNTE
ADAM HAAG
JG. 1926
EINGEWIESEN 1925
HEILANSTALT HERBORN
'VERLEGT' 12.3.1941
HADAMAR
ERMORDET 12.3.1941
AKTION T4

DESECRATION

GLORY DAYS

PENSIONERS

GLORY DAYS

PENSIONERS

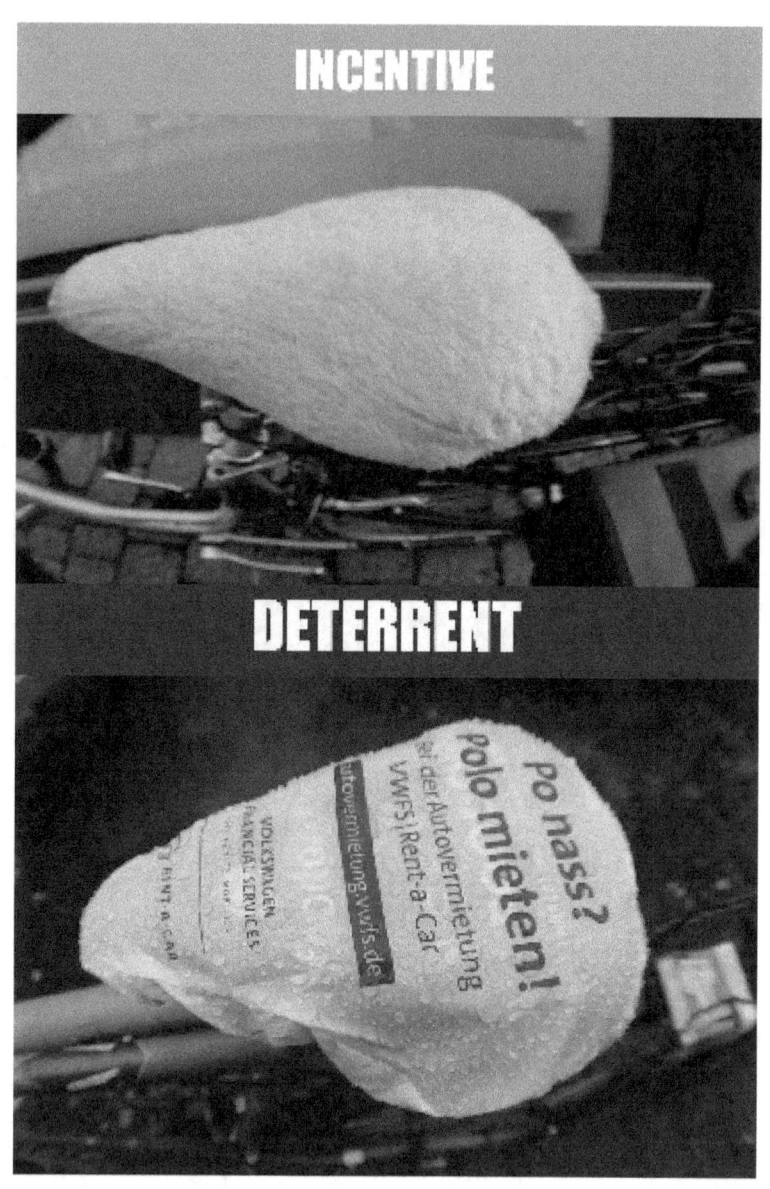

75

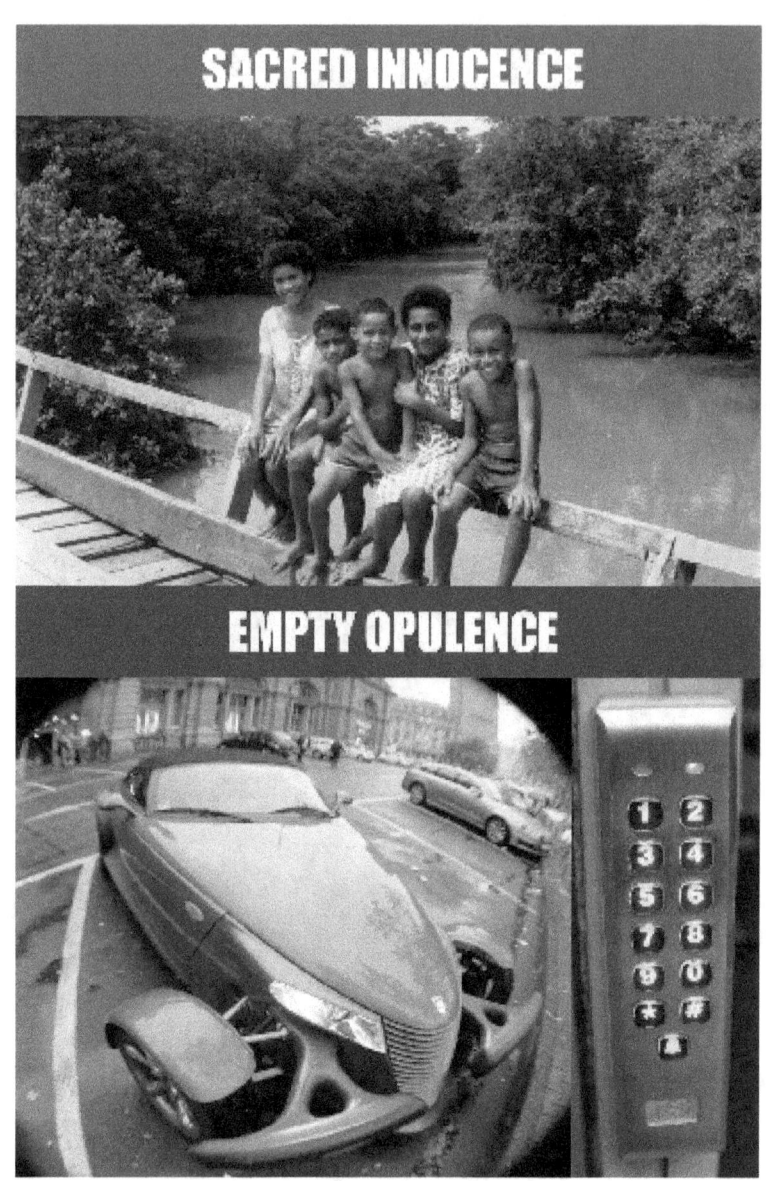

BEACHED SEA EQUIPMENT

PERMANENT BEACHED SEA CREATURE

TICKET MAGNET

WORRISOME CHOICE FOR A CAB DRIVER

SPLIT SECOND MISS

THE PATIENT BUS

96

ONE FOR THE ROAD

LAST CALL

In Loving Memory

MEREDITH CURLY HUNTER SR

BIG BUCK

OBSCENE BUCKS

USELESS IF DISASSEMBLED

USELESS IF GROUNDED

Author, photographer and visual artist Marques Vickers was born in 1957 in Vallejo, California. He graduated from Azusa Pacific University in Los Angeles and became the Public Relations and Executive Director for the Burbank, California Chamber of Commerce between 1979-84.

Professionally, he has operated travel, apparel, wine, rare book and publishing businesses. His paintings and sculptures have been exhibited in art galleries, private collections and museums in the United States and Europe. He has previously lived in the Burgundy and Languedoc regions of France and currently lives in the South Puget Sound region of Western Washington.

He has written and published over one hundred books spanning a diverse variety of subjects including true crime, international travel, social satire, wine production, architecture, history, fiction, auctions, fine art, poetry and photojournalism.

He has two daughters, Charline and Caroline who reside in Europe.

www.ingramcontent.com/pod-product-compliance
Lightning Source LLC
Chambersburg PA
CBHW070201290526
45789CB00002B/859